Horst Schulz

NEW KNITTING
Fashion for Children

Horst Schulz

NEW KNITTING
Fashion for
Children

Colourful, easy-to-knit patterns

Saprotex
International

Contents

Introduction

Let me help you to take a fresh look at knitting. Everything that surrounds us is made up of individual pieces. So why should knitting be any different?

A house is built brick by brick until the desired height is reached; floorboards are laid one alongside the other until the floor of a room is complete. I have constructed my knitting in exactly the same way – brick by brick or floorboard by floorboard = patch square by patch square = strip by strip. 'New knitting' is more than merely joining pieces together. However, it also involves the creative use of an endless variety of patterns, texture and colour.

You do not have to copy the designs and styles in this book exactly as shown. For a start, it will be difficult to find exactly the same yarns in exactly the same colours, as these change so frequently. Besides, I would like to re-awaken the creative streak we all have, In fact, I could even say that I am extending a challenge to all of you out there to tap into that hidden creativity – simply use your imagination, pick up those needles and get started!

The purpose of this book is to show you each respective knitting technique for making the individual pieces and the various possibilities for joining them. Trust your intuition when choosing colours and putting shapes together, and don't be afraid to experiment. The designs that my pupils and I knitted are shown here merely to encourage you to become creative yourselves.

It is my wish that people get together to exchange ideas and stimulate one another's interest, as happened in the spinning rooms and knitting circles in the past. These days, although we are bombarded by the electronic media, we lead rather isolated lives. Being creative is one way of feeding the soul.

Horst Schulz.

The Principles of patchwork knitting

The idea is simple and the result is remarkably effective: no more tangled threads while working with several balls of yarn. Our designs are created from single strips or square pieces which are joined together piece by piece whilst knitting. This means you only have a few stitches in one colour on your needle at any one time. The richness of colour is produced by changing the colour after one or several double rows. This knitting technique also has the advantage that the size of the knitted pieces can easily be adjusted. Children's garments can 'grow' at the same rate as the children by adding additional strips or pieces. If your knitting has turned out too big, you can take out individual strips. With the help of a paper pattern, you can check the size and shape whenever you want. As the coloured pieces are knitted individually, it is easy to correct the colours. If you have made a mistake in the colour, simply take out the piece and knit it again.

I assume you are already an experienced knitter, know how to cast on, and can knit stocking stitch and garter stitch. The technique of 'patchwork knitting' is based on these simple principles.

Casting on Stitches

When casting on it is better to use the two needle method as at a later stage you will often have only one thread available, so it is best to get used to this method right from the beginning.

The casting-on row always counts as the first row.

① *First make a loop.*

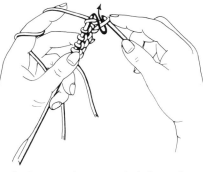

② *Cast on a new stitch from the first stitch and slip the new stitch backwards onto the left-hand needle.*

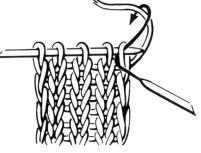

③ *Cast on the next stitch from the new stitch, slip it onto the left-hand needle, etc.*

④ *The stitches of the caston row will appear as in the diagram above.*

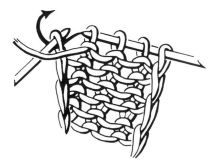

⑤ *Shown above is an example of new stitches being cast on from an edge stitch.*

Edge Stitches

Edge stitches are very important for 'Patchwork knitting'. You need them to join individual strips or pieces. You can only join the pieces neatly if the edge stitches are worked evenly. The drawings show you how to knit the edge stitches. For every two rows worked (= 1 double row) one edge stitch is produced in the shape of a "V" on both sides.

① *Always work the 1st stitch of each row knitwise, or knitwise into the back of the stitch.*

② *Always slip purlwise the last stitch of each row with the yarn in front.*

My tip:

If the edge stitches become very loose, you can still tighten the yarn: knit the second stitch, then pull yarn tighter. When changing colour

you should always take the second thread behind the first thread. Then the edge stitches will remain correct and be easily visible.

Weaving in the ends of Threads

The weaving in of the ends of threads is an absolute must when working with an endless variety of colour. It is easier than you may think, and saves you the bother of sewing them in after you have finished the work. You can weave in one to three ends at a time (7–10 cm long) on the reverse side if you knit on the front side and purl on the reverse side (=stocking stitch). By using this method – one over, one under – you can carry sideways threads from the second stitch next to the edge stitch. With moss stitch you can weave in threads on both sides. If you knit on both sides (=garter stitch), you can weave in the ends by laying it along the back of your work. Weaving in does not work with rows of slip stitches. You can only do this one or two rows later

Drawing 1 and 2 show you how to weave in the ends for rows of knit stitches, drawings 3 and 4 for rows of purl stitches.

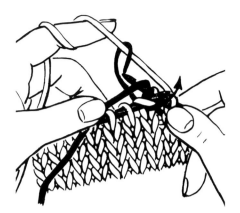

① *Hold the end of the thread with thumb and middle finger of your left hand. Insert the needle into the stitch on the front side, place the thread which is to be woven in over the right-hand needle, and knit the stitch only with the working thread.*

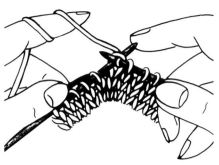

② *Hold the end of the thread with thumb and middle finger of your left hand. Insert the needle into the stitch on the front side, place the thread which is to be woven in under the right-hand needle, and knit the stitch only with the working thread.*

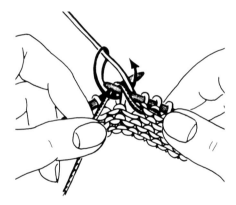

③ *Hold the end of the thread with thumb and middle finger of your left hand. Place the thread which is to be woven in over the right-hand needle and purl the stitch only with the working threads.*

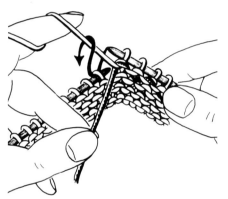

④ *Hold the end of the thread with thumb and middle finger of your left hand. Place the thread which is to be woven in under the right-hand needle and purl the stitch only with the working thread.*

Knitting strips together

There are two methods of knitting the strips together. According to the method chosen, you can see the two adjoining rows of stitches either on the front or the reverse side.

Technique I: see diagram 1
Joining strip B to strip A knitwise

1. On strip B, slip the last stitch knitwise.
2. Pick up and knit a corresponding stitch from the side of strip A.
3. Pass slip stitch over this stitch.
4. Turn work and with yarn in front, slip the 1st stitch purlwise. Purl across row.

5. The result will be two rows of parallel stitches.

Technique II: see diagram 2
Joining strip B to strip A purlwise

1. On strip B slip the last stitch purlwise.
2. Pick up and purl corresponding

stitch from the side of strip A.

3. Slip last 2 stitches onto left hand needle and purl these 2 stitches together.

4. Turn work and slip 1st stitch knitwise. Knit across row.

Technique III: see diagram 3

For many patterns I recommend you knit the strips together with a circular needle. To do so first pick up and knit new stitches on a circular needle from all the right-hand edge stitches of the finished strip=strip A. Now you do not have to spend a long time searching for the edge stitches, as you already have them on your needle. Of course, you can start knitting a few rows up and down with these stitches. Then cast on strip B with the right needle of a circular needle, and take the yarn in front of the knitting. Now again, as before, purl together the left edge stitch of strip B and the first stitch on the circular needle. On the reverse row take the yarn behind the knitting and slip the first stitch knitwise.

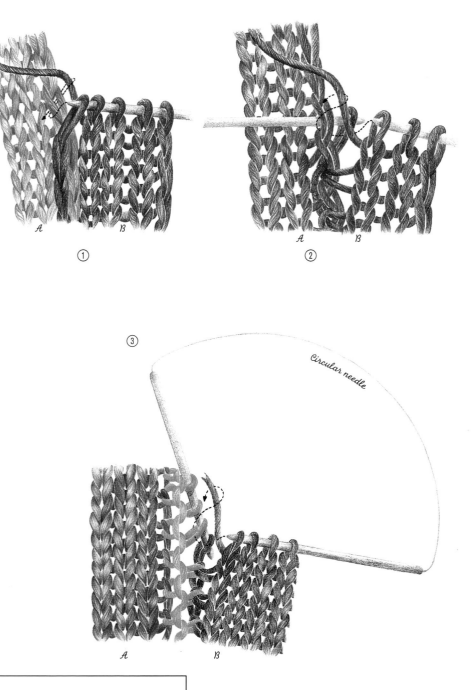

My tip:

Dark colours make it difficult to recognise the edge stitches easily. Using a light background, a white tablecloth or a piece of paper can be very useful.

Joining patches using the 'Square' method

Besides working in strips you can also work with smaller pieces, and knit them together as in patchwork. The square with the diagonally decreasing stitches produces surprising patterns and in addition leaves a lot of scope for your own creativity. Just make sure that when you knit the stitches of each square together (=decrease), you do this only in the middle of the return rows.

To knit according to the 'square' method first complete a square. In our examples a double row of garter stitch is knitted alternately with a double row of stocking stitch. The next square is knitted from the previous one by picking up half of the stitches from the existing edge, and by casting on the other half of the stitches. In this way strips are formed. You can also stand the squares on their points: then

instead of working in the usual strips technique, use the patchwork technique.

The single square
The diagram shows how the shape is made and in the sequence which they are knitted together.

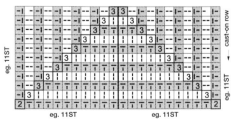

The double square
The diagram shows how a double square is made.

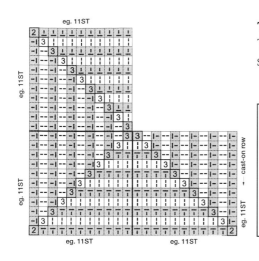

The triple square

The diagram shows how the triple square is made.

My tip:

When knitting a triple square it is advisable to knit one square first as this makes it clearer as to how you should continue the work.

The quadruple square

The quadruple square is an important variation. Cast on at an outer edge and knit towards the middle in rows. The open edges can lead from the middle of one side to the middle of the piece (drawing 1 and photograph bottom right), or from one corner to the middle of the piece (drawing 2). In both cases the edges must be sewn or knitted together neatly. To do this, pick up new stitches with the working yarn from the edge stitches of both sides using a needle or circular needle for each edge. On one edge knit from the middle to the corner, and on the other edge knit from the corner to the middle and loosely cast off the stitches with a third needle from the middle to the corner, as shown in drawing 3.

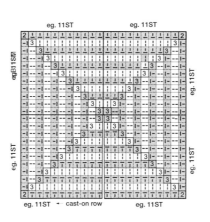

Drawing 1

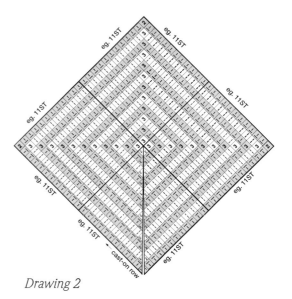

Drawing 2

Drawing 3

My tip:

On the edge of the quadruple square, knit the last two stitches of the return row, and then slip the edge stitch purlwise with the yarn in front as described above. In the forward row knit these two stitches together. In this way a 'V'- shaped edge stitch is maintained for this double row.

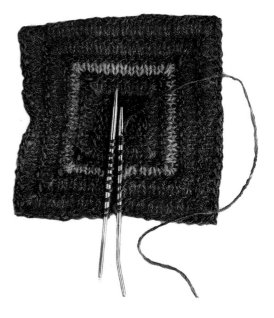

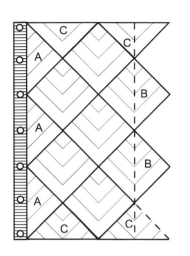

The half square

A) Often half squares have to be made at the side margins in order to give a straight finish to diamond shaped patches.

B) You do not have to sew two half-squares together at the seam – you can also work 'seamlessly'. Make a complete square instead of two halves, fold it where the seam would be, and use it for joining or sewing the square on the other side.

C)To finish off straight edges at the upper and lower margins, knit half squares 'with their heads chopped off' as follows: knit each individual square according to the pattern, except at the beginning of each row: knit the first two stitches into the back of the stitch. Cast off the last four to five stitches at once. This keeps the knitting straight and prevents it from bulging.

The paper pattern

Before you pick up your needles you need to have a paper pattern of the desired garment. As most of the garments shown here are based on rectangles or squares, this paper pattern has been made up accordingly. It does not matter whether you are knitting something for an adult or a child. By using his or her own pullover or jacket you can easily make a pattern for an individual size. You can check the state of your work at any time with this original-sized paper pattern: simply place the pre-stretched knitting over it. Then you can easily see how many strips or pieces are needed to finish the

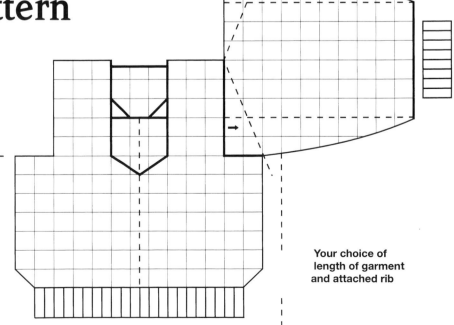

Your choice of length of garment and attached rib

garment. For the shaped parts of the sleeves you can either knit the shaped piece onto the finished piece, or knit on the whole piece right away using the paper pattern. The straight edges of the shoulder pieces can be folded back from each side of the centre at a slight angle, and then sewn: usually a small shoulder pad is placed under the seam later.

My tip:

Stretch out the pieces of knitting carefully. You can only determine the exact size and see the complete beauty of the knitting when it is stretched out.

The trick with the mirror

If, after a short time and with a relatively small piece of knitting, you would like to see the effect a larger piece of knitting will give, then use a mirror. Put one edge of your knitting against the mirror and you can already see the continuation of your work in the reflection (photograph below). This little trick gives you a preview of your work and encourages you to continue.

Knitting the rib

In the 'old way of knitting' you always started each piece with the rib. In 'patchwork knitting' the ribs are knitted right at the end. To keep them in better shape it is advisable to knit them double.

It is best to start with a sleeve, then you can quickly see how many stitches produce how many centimetres of knitting. I usually use yarn with a length of about 100 m per 50 gm ball of yarn. As a rule of thumb about 40-44 stitches are needed for a sleeve, and about 80 stitches for both the front and back piece. Children's garments require slightly less.

For a rib, first knit all the stitches on the inside part of the piece onto a circular needle. In the second row you must now decrease to the required number of stitches or increase the stitches (make a stitch by picking up

the horizontal loop before the next stitch and knitting into the back of it). Continue knitting until the desired length is reached, then purl one row for the turning ridge of the hem and continue according to the pattern selected. Cast off the stitches very loosely (about 1 cm for every stitch) so that a row of purl appears on the front side. Now simply fold back the rib and sew loosely onto the front side in slip stitch. The cast-off row of stitches and the turning ridge for the hem should stretch as much as the knitted part does.

Slip stitches make the rib especially firm. Knit to the turning ridge for the hem as described above. Then continue knitting according to illustration 1 and 2. It is best to use needles half a size bigger because now you often knit only every other stitch. It also looks good if you use a somewhat thicker yarn for the second colour. The rib can

also be knitted in several different colours: if rib patterns are alternately knitted 1 st knit, 1 st purl, or 2 sts knit, 2 sts purl with slip stitches, they will not curl up. Start immediately with the pattern, but do not knit the reverse or inside in stocking stitch. When you have finished knitting the row in the first colour do not turn it around. Start from the beginning again with the second yarn (illustrations 3 and 4). The yarn of the first colour should be somewhat thicker here. A wonderful pattern for the rib is produced by knitting 4 rows of slip stitches. Alternately knit two rows in the first colour and four rows in the second colour (illustration 5).

The number of stitches for the rib should be divisible by four, with two additional stitches left over. You will get a neat join if you start and finish the row with two purl stitches.

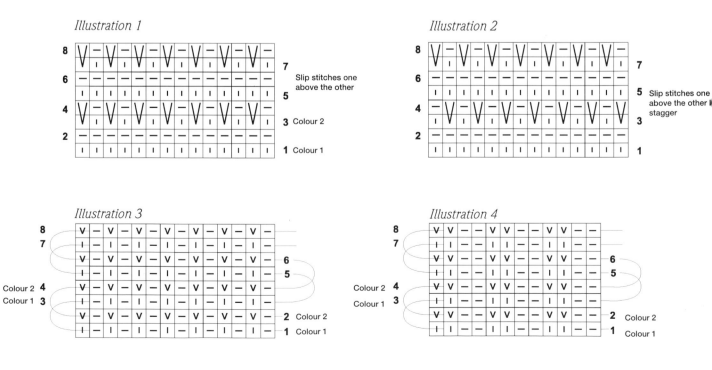

Illustration 5

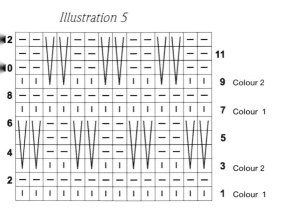

For children's models it is best to knit the rib in moss stitch with a somewhat thicker yarn.

It is easier to knit the bands of the jacket by working in three parts. The two front bands and the neck. Then it is quite easy to check, – and if necessary, to correct – whether the right number of stitches has been increased and if the dimensions are in order. Finally sew the three separate parts neatly together. If you cannot find any details about the rib in the description of the models presented here, select one of the pattern variations described here and choose the corresponding colours for it. Another important piece of advice before you select a design: pay attention to the structure and suitability of the pattern.

Note: Not every yarn is suitable for every pattern. Make a small pattern and material sample and test for suitability and visual effect. That will ensure the ultimate success of your work.

Explanation of symbols

Casting on

Cast on stitches using the two needle cast-on method

| ı | | Knit 1 stitch |
| - | | Purl 1 stitch |

Attention:

The symbols on the illustration are given as the stitches appear on the front side.

2. Row 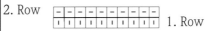 1. Row

ie knit the 1st and 2nd row so that you have purl stitches on the front. The result is a garter stitch pattern. The same applies for knitting stitches together. When knitting two stitches together, knit them together through the back of loop and when purling two stitches together, purl them together through back of loop.
For stitch patterns with an uneven number of stitches, knit continuously 1 knit, 1 purl. The result will be moss stitch on both sides.
An odd number of stitches always gives the same rhythm of stitches on both sides.
For moss stitch patterns you can knit pieces together as the pattern determines.

Attention:

The edge stitches are not counted extra. Knit the first stitch. Slip the last stitch purlwise (see page 7)
Always begin the rows at the number of the row indicated in the illustration.

Each new piece always starts on the right side (front side) with a row of knit stitches.

SQ	Square
ST	Stitch
R	Row
DR	Double Row ie knit one row forward and one row back
DEC	Decrease
INC	Increase
2 -	Purl 2 stitches together
2 ı	Knit 2 stitches together into the backs of the stitches
3 -	Purl 3 stitches together
3 ı	Knit 3 stitches together into the backs of the stitches
⊼	Instead of knitting next stitch, pick up next stitch from one row below and knit it.
V	1 slip stitch, ie slip one stitch as you would purl, taking the working yarn along behind on the front side, and in front on the reverse side.
◢	From the yarn between two stitches knit a new stitch into the back of the stitch (to prevent holes)
⋈	Cable 2 stitches
⊞	Cable 4 stitches

Model
Gallery

Child's jacket with car buttons

We shall begin with a very simple pattern. It is a wonderful opportunity to practise weaving in the ends of yarn.

Always make sure your edge stitches are the same size.

Before starting work, prepare an original-sized paper pattern made out of strong brown paper according to your desired measurements (see page 12).

For every strip cast on 13 stitches using the two needle method and knit in moss stitch. The second and each subsequent strip is attached to each other as shown in the illustration by knitting together according to technique 1 (see page 8). The interesting structure of the colours is achieved by a 'magic ball of wool' which is made as follows:

Cut strips, about 50 cm to 100 cm long, in different colours of light yarn, and strips about 1 m to 3 m long in different colours of dark yarn. Knot the longer and shorter pieces alternately with a weaver's knot. To do this, hold one end of yarn in each hand. Lay the right thread end under the left on (drawing 1) and hold both of them tight in the left hand between thumb and forefinger. Now loop the right thread around the thumb of the left hand behind the left and in front of the

right thread end. Take the left thread end behind, and hold it tight with the middle finger. Insert the right end through the loop which is on the left thumb (arrow drawing 2). Afterwards tighten the loop by pulling with the right hand.

By using a very thin decorative yarn with the yarn you are knitting, and by winding both yarns together, you will balance out the colour change. This change of colour produces an 'intended coincidence' which makes this design particularly attractive.

Finally pick up the stitches for the ribs in moss stitch from the inner side (wrong side facing). A similar effect will be produced as if you had knitted the stitches because the edge stitch is visible on the front side. Work with a double thread. Choose a finishing colour for the vertical bands. With right side facing knit one row then cast off loosely on the next row.

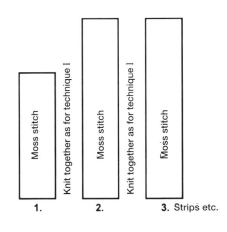

Child's jacket with strawberry buttons

This garment is made in the same way as the jacket with car buttons previously described. However, make your 'magic ball of wool' from threads of about 3 m long, or change the colour after each six double rows.

Child's pullover with slip stitches

This pullover is also made up of individual strips. The strips are knitted in different patterns with the same sequence of colours, always one double row in a dark foundation colour alternating with two double rows in strong pastel colours.

For pattern 1 work one double row of garter stitch (10 stitches) and for pattern 2 work one double row of garter stitch (16 stitches) and follow the pattern with slip stitches. Continue repeating rows 1 to 12. Match up the strips colour-wise, and knit them together using the same method as described in technique 111 (see page 9). This pullover can easily be turned into a short-sleeve pullover by sewing zips into the armholes.

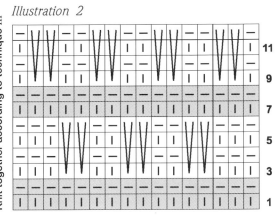

Illustration 1   *Illustration 2*

Knit together according to technique III

Child's jacket with slanting strips

Begin by casting on two stitches at the bottom corner (2 ST). To produce the shape, increase 1 stitch on both sides of each double row until you have 21 stitches on your needle. Knit 2 stitches together at the beginning of each forward row after the edge stitch, and pick up one stitch from the yarn between two stitches at

the end of each forward row before the edge stitch.

To continue the pattern, knit 6 double rows alternately in moss stitch in one colour (colour 1) and 4 double rows (2 x slip stitch) in another colour (colour 2). You can also 'play' by using two shades of the same colour in the same square. The strips are knitted together according to technique III (see page 9) to form a diagonal pattern.

Attention – the following rule must be observed at all costs: when working with these slanting strips the relationship of row to length no longer applies. The length is now measured in centimetres.

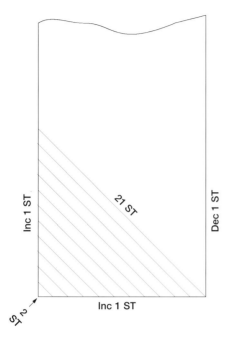

Inc 1 ST

21 ST

Dec 1 ST

Inc 1 ST

2 ST

Explanation of strips and cables

Cables can also be knitted in strips with different variations and colours and attached to other strips. Our example is knitted together according to technique III with three double rows garter stitch. For each cable strip cast on 10 stitches using the two needle method. The illustration shows you how to continue knitting. In the return rows (not shown) knit the stitches as they appear. Repeat with rows 1–10.

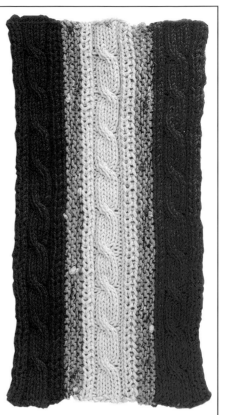

Knit as many cable strips together as your pattern shows. Finally attach the ribs (see pages 14–15)

There are no limits to your imagination. You can also alter the cables as much as you wish.

This means that after taking up the edge stitches with a circular needle from the right-hand edge of strip A, for the second row you should alternately knit two stitches, then pick up a stitch from the yarn between two threads. Knit rows 3 to 7 as shown in the illustration. In the 8th row alternately purl 2 stitches together, and purl one stitch. This prevents the strip from puckering diagonally and producing unsightly wrinkles. The next diagonal strip is knitted together according to technique III immediately after the 2 casting-on stitches with the stitches of the diagonally knitted strip from the circular needle. In this way the strips are placed together until the required width of the knitting has been reached. The ribs are knitted in moss stitch as for the garment on page 17, only here the stitches are picked up on the front side.

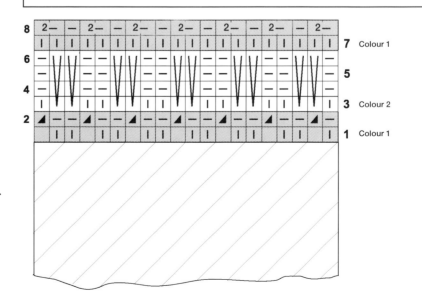

Jacket in
squares for
young and
old

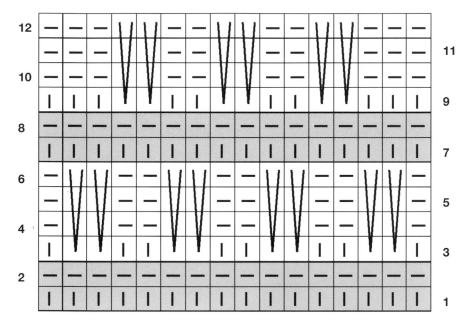

Small jacket:
For one strip cast on 16 stitches using the two needle method. Start the pattern by knitting 24 rows (12 double rows) in any two colours. Continue the pattern by repeating the 24 rows in any two different colours.

Here the interesting structure of the fabric is splendidly complemented by the different qualities of yarn and colour. The rows of slip stitches are knitted with hard-wearing sock wool. Underneath these you can see the coloured squares of fleecy mohair wool. Both jackets are made by knitting together vertical strips as in technique II (see pages 8–9). The illustration shows the details of the stitches. The number of stitches must be divisible by 4. The size is taken from the paper pattern.

Large jacket:
For one strip cast on 24 stitches using the two needle method. Start the pattern by knitting 30 rows (15 double rows) in any two colours. Continue the pattern by repeating the 30 rows in any two different colours.

Child's jacket with hood

With this special cable pattern the strips are formed by alternately attaching the squares horizontally and vertically. For the first vertical cable piece cast on 17 stitches and knit as follows: in each return row alternately slip one stitch yarn over needle and knit one stitch, in each forward row; alternately knit one stitch with yarn over needle, and purl the next stitch. If that is too complicated just knit one colour squares in any simple pattern. The darker colour in the first double row creates contrasts. Here 34 rows (17 double rows) are knitted for each pattern. The cabling is done in the 18th row. Finish the piece with a double row of garter stitch in a darker yarn.

For the next horizontal cable piece cast on 17 new stitches on the left upper edge of the first piece. The second piece is knitted together with the first piece as in technique I (see page 8).

Make sure that you knit the squares together only on the reserve side. The next vertical square is picked up from the previous one.

If the first complete strip is made out of cable squares, pick up new stitches with the dark colour from each edge stitch from the right to make the intermediary strip, and knit a return row. Then knit a double row of slip stitches in a different colour, and another double row garter stitch with a dark yarn. Now make the strip by adding more cable squares to the first strip which you have already made. The squares in a vertical direction are knitted together with the stitches of the intermediary strip as in technique III (see page 9), the squares in a horizontal direction are joined by picking up stitches from the stitches of the intermediary strips. The garment shown on page 25 should fit sizes 1–2 years. The diagram shows the number of squares, the direction for knitting and how many strips are needed for one piece.

The photograph shows both this jacket and the child's pullover with coloured shapes as described on page 54.

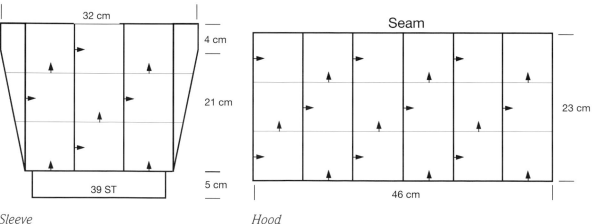

Sleeve

Hood

Child's jacket with herringbone strips

This design is made according to the herringbone method described on the left. Knit any number of double rows in moss stitch, then a double row of garter stitch, a double row of slip stitches, and a double row of garter stitch. You can arrange the colours in a set fashion, or make multicoloured strips using leftover yarn. By leaving the edges of the single squares open at the bottom you get a decorative finish.

Explanation of herringbone pattern

This pattern offers you the next decorative variation of the strip technique. Each strip begins with 23 stitches. Knit alternately a double row of garter stitch and a double row of stocking stitch. In each forward row knit one stitch from the yarn between two stitches at the beginning after the edge stitch and at the end before the edge stitch. In each return row knit or purl the 3 middle stitches together through back of loop. The second and each following strip are knitted together as in technique I (see page 8). If the coloured threads have crossed in the middle of the strip, knit the forward rows in the first colour up to and including the middle stitch, and then continue in the second colour. In the return rows knit the 3 stitches together with the thread which you happen to have in your hand.

Explanation of strips and squares

This example is a free composition made up of strips and small squares. For the strips knit alternately one double row garter stitch in colour 1, and a double row stocking stitch in colour 2 using the 'magic ball' (see page 17). Start the squares with the 'magic ball' (colour 2). The work can be done straight or diagonally

Brick jacket

Brick by brick – the jacket is soon finished. Start the jacket as for the squares, only with unequal sides. Cast on 18 plus 7 stitches for the light 'mortar' colour. Knit a return row in purl. To form the corner, purl 2 stitches together. Next knit the brick along the 17 stitches of the longer side 1 – one double row garter stitch and 5 double rows in moss stitch in a reddish yarn. Brick and mortar are knitted together according to technique III (see page 9). After a total of 7 double rows, cast off in purl on

the reverse side. The bricks are staggered like a real brick wall.

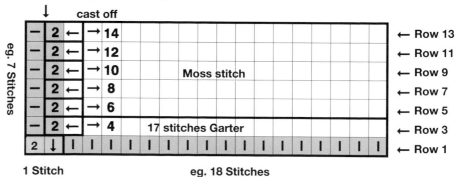

Knit together on a circular needle as explained (technique III)

Jackets in Patchwork style

This classic patchwork pattern is also a combination of strips and squares. The pieces are knitted in moss stitch and the strips are knitted together according to technique II (see pages 8–9). The diagram shows the simple laying of strips together. Start by casting on 17 stitches (8 ST + 1 middle stitch + 8 ST) using the two needle method. Now knit 9 stitches in colour 1 and 8 stitches in colour 2. Cross over the yarns when changing colour. On the reverse side, knit the 3 middle stitches together. On the front side, at the beginning of the row after the edge stitch and at the end of the row before the edge stitch, pick up one stitch from the yarn between two threads. Knit 8 double rows. Then cast on 8 stitches for each side using the two needle method, or else pick up stitches later from other existing pieces. Now knit another 8 double rows of 33 stitches

(16 ST + 1 middle stitch + 16 ST). Continue knitting with colour 3 without increasing any more stitches at the sides (see page 10, squares) until the number of stitches has been reduced once again to 17. Now knit the next piece in a different colour combination. You do not, therefore,

have to knit with more than two colours at a time to produce this colourful piece. Make sure that the colour shades dark-medium-light are always placed in the same order to produce a three-dimensional effect.

The diagram below should fit children aged 4 years.

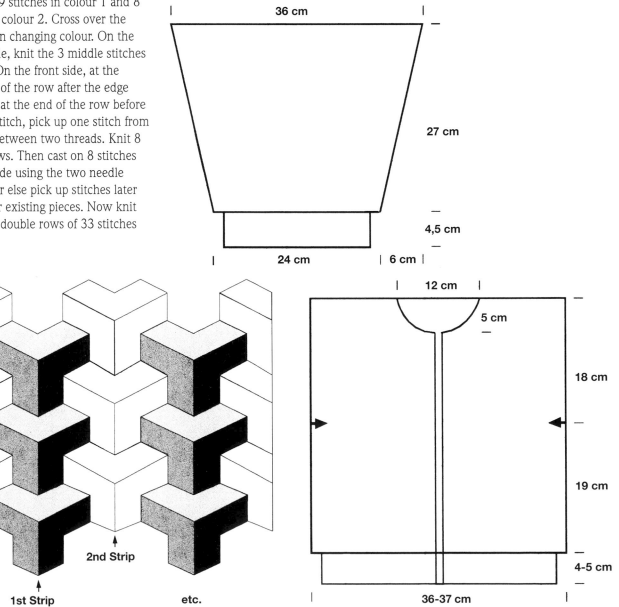

36 cm

27 cm

4,5 cm

24 cm   6 cm

1/2 Strip   2nd Strip

1st Strip   etc.

12 cm

5 cm

18 cm

19 cm

4-5 cm

36-37 cm

Two small diamond jackets

Both these jackets are easily knitted in single squares of garter stitch (see page 10) which are placed on their points. For the first jacket, dark blue squares alternate with turquoise ones, while the first double row of each square is always knitted in white. The jacket is made simply by joining coloured pieces, the first two double rows of each are always knitted in a foundation colour.

Child's multi-coloured jacket

The interesting effect of this jacket is produced by the staggered arrangement of the double squares. For each square knit alternately 1 double row garter and 1 double row stocking stitch. The material used here is sock wool, colour 1 = multicolour, colour 2 = solid colour, (but in different shades). Knit the double squares as indicated on page 10.

Explanation of windmills

This variation brings a fresh breeze into the knitting landscape. The wonderful effect is produced quite simply by knitting together squares with a change of colour in the diagonal. For each square cast on 11 stitches in colour 1 and 11 stitches in colour 2 and knit these back to back. Knit with colour 2 in the return row as described on page 10 for the 'single squares' and at the middle change and continue knitting with colour 1. When changing colour always cross the threads! The individual squares are knitted together to form long strips, each time by picking up half of the stitches from existing squares or by casting on new stitches. The solid vertical bars in the diagram mark the places where the following strip is joined to the previous one using technique II (see pages 8 to 9).

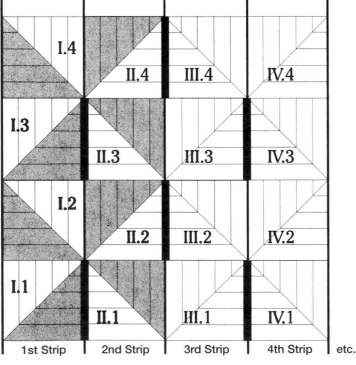

I.4 II.4 III.4 IV.4

I.3 II.3 III.3 IV.3

I.2 II.2 III.2 IV.2

I.1 II.1 III.1 IV.1

1st Strip   2nd Strip   3rd Strip   4th Strip   etc.

Jacket with a scale pattern

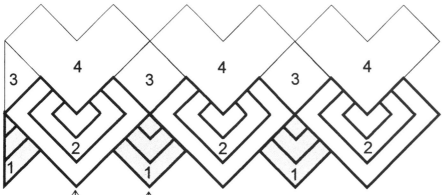

Triple
square

Individual
square

joined to each other. Between these individual squares the 'triple-squares' are placed. The joining is done by taking up stitches from the existing edges of the individual squares. In the third row, individual squares are inserted between triple squares, and in the fourth row the 'triple-squares' are inserted again, etc.

The diagram shows the arrangement of the squares. For one side of a square cast on 11 stitches or pick them up (see pages 7, 10, 11). To finish off the work, fill in the edges at the sides with half-squares at the top and with folded over squares at the bottom (see page 12). You can leave the lower edge pointed or add a rib.

In this example 'single' and 'triple' squares stand on their points. Begin the jacket at the bottom edge with a corresponding number of individual squares (see diagram) which are not

Jacket with squares for father and son

This imaginative jacket is made with a daring use of colour and by putting together 'triple' and 'quadruple' squares (see page 11). The materials used are different kinds of sock wool and kid-mohair. The 'triple-squares' are knitted in moss stitch, each side having 11 stitches.

The 'quadruple-squares' are knitted in garter stitch, each side having 11 stitches. The diagram suggests how the pieces could be arranged. The cute child's jacket is knitted following the same principle as the gents jacket, only with a different combination of colours.

My tip:

Carefully stretch out smaller pieces at the beginning, then again at different stages of your knitting. This makes it easier for you to compare the size.

Child's waistcoat

This child's waistcoat is another variation of 'triple' and 'quadruple' squares (see page 11). The 'triple-square' technique differs insofar as the knitting together of the stitches on the reverse side is not done exactly in the middle, but completely at random. This produces a roundish shape. The moss stitch pattern makes the colours flow softly into one another. As an aid I attach a safety-pin at the beginning of each of the three corners in order to

mark the places where I have to decrease stitches. The material is a 'magic ball' made up of leftover yarn (see page 17).

Here the individual pieces are about 50 to 70 cm long. The ends of the yarn are

immediately woven in on the reverse side. This is a really exciting piece of knitting as you cannot predict what it will look like when it is finished. It consists entirely of leftover yarn to which I have added a thin secondary thread.

Short-sleeve jacket for girls

The knitting technique for this jacket is very similar to that of the child's waistcoat on pages 40 and 41. Again, round-shaped 'triple squares' which have been knitted from a 'magic ball' are imaginatively put together, but here the 'quadruple squares' in-between have been omitted

Gents jacket with diagonal strips

The interesting diagonal pattern is produced by knitting diagonal strips and inserting 'single' and 'quadruple' squares in-between as shown in the diagram. Sock-wool and kid-mohair were used.

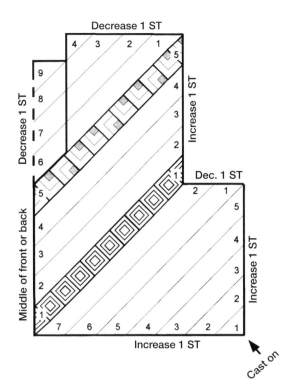

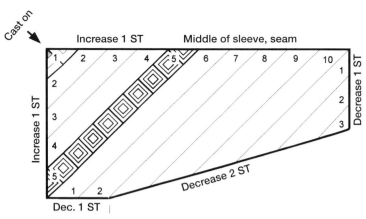

The illustration below shows the pattern with slip stitches. Change the colour at random for rows 7 to 10: this makes the result more lively. When changing colour, join the thread of the new colour to the previous thread with a simple knot. In the rows of slip stitches it is not possible to weave in the threads, so this is done in the next double row of garter stitch. Start the jacket by casting on 3 stitches at the corner, both for the front as well as the back piece. Then one stitch is increased on both sides in each double row until the desired width has been reached. At the front edges, at the horizontal edge for sleeve, neck and shoulder decrease by 1 stitch in each double row. Begin each sleeve-half at the corner, again with 3 stitches, and then increase by one stitch on both sides in each double row until the desired width has been reached. Continue increasing on the left hand side of work (= edge of middle of sleeve) to the lower edge (= cuff) then decrease one stitch. At the side edge of the sleeve, first decrease 1 stitch in each double row, then decrease 2 stitches for the tapering of the sleeves. On the model shown 42 stitches were picked up for the rib of the sleeve, and 172 stitches for the lower rib (42 stitches for the front, 88 stitches for the back, 42 stitches for the front). Pick up 9 stitches from each strip for the bands, and about 30 stitches for the neck. The seams at the sides, middle of back, shoulders, and middle of the sleeve are then sewn together.

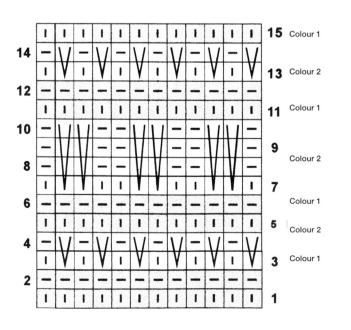

Child's jacket with diagonal strips

This child's jacket (see photograph on page 43) is the smaller version of the larger gents jacket. Correspondingly, it has just one strip of 'quadruple' squares inserted, and is knitted entirely out of sock wool.

Baby's jacket
with diagonal strips

All good things come in three's. This is the smallest pattern made according to the previous principle. Only here the squares knitted in-between the strips have been left out completely. Again, sock wool was used. The rows of slip stitches are your own free design, and the slip stitches are arranged off-centre.

Child's jacket made with 'quadruple squares'

'Quadruple squares' knitted together in a straight line with a change of colour in the middle of the square give a wonderful effect to this little jacket. When changing colour cross the threads on the reverse side.

Sketch the individual pieces on your paper pattern giving the corresponding indication of colour. In this way you can always see which colours you have to knit next. Add the ribs at the end in a colour that matches the dark wool in the middle of the square.

Child's jacket with a kite pattern

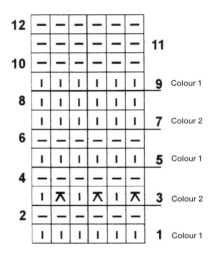

12	−	−	−	−	−	−		
	−	−	−	−	−	−	11	
10	−	−	−	−	−	−		
	I	I	I	I	I	I	9	Colour 1
8	I	I	I	I	I	I		
	I	I	I	I	I	I	7	Colour 2
6	−	−	−	−	−	−		
	I	I	I	I	I	I	5	Colour 1
4	−	−	−	−	−	−		
	I	⊼	I	⊼	I	⊼	3	Colour 2
2	−	−	−	−	−	−		
	I	I	I	I	I	I	1	Colour 1

The colourful children's jackets on this and the following page are made up of quadruple squares that look like small kites. The yarn used is sock wool. Start at the upper edge. The diagram shows the arrangement of the pieces for the front. You can make the edges of the front and back piece straight by filling in with half squares, or you can knit complete squares at the edge and use these immediately for knitting on the next piece of the jacket. The pattern for each square is made by working into the stitch in the row below as shown in the illustration. The colours are changed every double row, but the last two double rows are knitted in one colour. The formation of the shape is made by following the description of the quadruple squares on page 11 and by following the diagram on this page. Knit stitches together only on the return rows. For each square cast on 44 stitches.

The knitting together at the end with 3 needles is done from the middle to the corner of each piece with the same number of stitches on both sides, and by casting off loosely at the same time.

Start the work

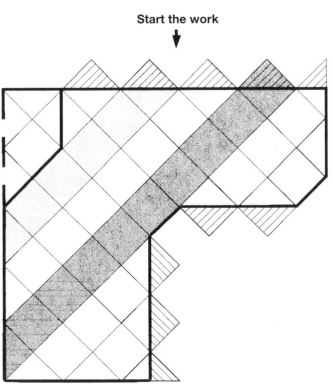

Gents jacket with kite pattern

The gents jacket in somewhat toned-down colours is also knitted according to the same principle as the child's jacket. The sleeves are fitted with zips so that the jacket can also be worn as a waistcoat. Sock wool and kid-mohair have been used. Select any three similar shades of colour from your stock of wool for this design. Each square starts on the two middle sides with a double row of garter stitch in one of the three colours. For the first row cast on 24 stitches using the two needle method.

In the second row knit 10 stitches, knit 2 stitches together twice, and knit another 10 stitches. For the third row cast on 11 stitches. Knit 11 stitches twice, and cast on 11 stitches again in the colour sequence according to the diagram. You now have 44 stitches

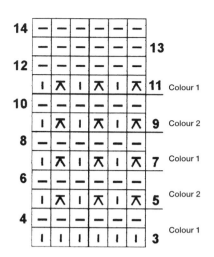

on your needle. Continue knitting the square as described on pages 11 and 48.

Child's pullover with coloured pencils

For this pullover pencil strips are placed side by side according to technique III (see page 9). Depending on whether the following strips are to be joined on the right or the left side, knit them together either at the end of the forward row or at the end of the return row. Begin the pencil numbers, 1, 4, 6, etc from the bottom, and the numbers 2, 3, 5, 7, etc from the top. After each pencil has been completed, work the borders in a darker colour in the sequence (forward and back) as shown in the drawing. The yarn used has a length of ± 135 m per 50 g. Cast on 11 stitches for each pencil strip, and knit as follows: 3 stitches moss stitch, 1 stitch st st, 3 stitches moss stitch, 1 stitch st st, 3 stitches moss stitch. This is just a suggestion, and a simpler pattern can be used if you desire. For the points, knit or purl two stitches together in every third row on both sides. The points can be marked in colour by embroidering them in coloured stitches.

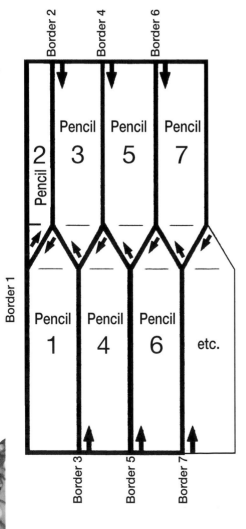

Child's pull-over with coloured shapes

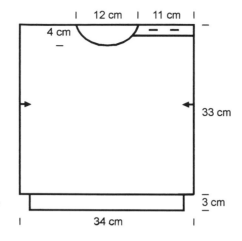
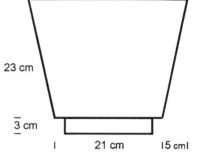

12 cm | 11 cm

4 cm

33 cm

34 cm

3 cm

31 cm

23 cm

3 cm

21 cm | 5 cm

The coloured shapes on this pullover are arranged like towers of building blocks. Yarn with a length of 125 m per 50 gm was used. The coloured shapes are knitted in moss stitch. Begin each square with unequal sides (see brick jacket, page 28). Knit the first double row in garter stitch with the dark contrasting colour. Continue with the strips according to the technique used for the brick jacket but arranging the shapes in different directions. The ribs are worked with slip stitches in a darker contrast colour with remnants of multicolour sock wool in-between. Cast on 146 stitches for the bottom rib, and 40 stitches for each sleeve rib.

This diagram is an illustration of how the shapes can be arranged. The pattern should fit children of about 2 years of age.

68 edge stitches

The child's jacket with a hood on page 24 compliments this pullover.

Child's jacket with cubes

For this jacket a popular patchwork pattern has found its use in knitting. Each cube consists of three parts: the two front sides and the 'lid' as the upper square. Cast on 19 stitches for each front side. The pattern for all the cubes is the same – one double row stocking stitch, one double row garter stitch. In each forward row at the beginning, after the edge stitch, and at the end before the edge stitch, increase by one stitch by picking up the loop

Pattern

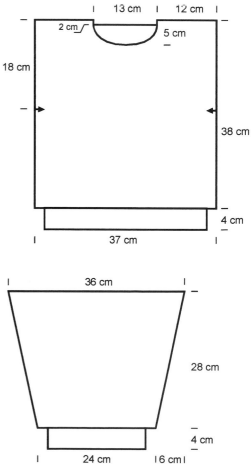

Pattern design 1

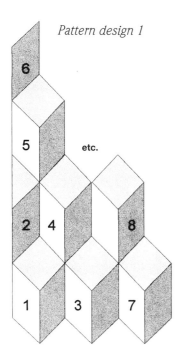

Pattern design 2

the middle stitch in the first colour, and then continue in the second colour. In the return rows knit together the three stitches with the thread you happen to have in your hand. For the top of the cube continue working with the stitches from the right-hand front side. Knit without increasing or decreasing the stitches. On the left edge the square is knitted purlwise with another finished piece according to technique III (see page 9). The sequence of the individual pieces is based completely on patchwork as diagram I shows. Knit half-cubes to make a straight finish to the edges. Knit 140 stitches for the lower rib, and 40 stitches for the sleeve rib. According to diagram 2, experienced knitters can also knit a large design on the back. The jacket was made up from many remnants of wool with a length of 125 m per 50 gm. This garment should fit children aged 3 to 4 years old.

between the stitches and knitting into the back of the stitch.

In each return row the middle 3

stitches are knitted or purled into the back of the stitch according to the pattern. Using this technique the number of stitches remains unchanged, and a kind of 'V' is produced. Should the coloured threads become crossed in the middle just knit up to and including

Explanation of cubes

This is another variation when knitting cubes. A completely different effect is produced if you use knobbly yarn. For both front pieces cast on 23 stitches.

Child's jacket with shell pattern

Of course knitting single pieces together also works with shapes other than strips or squares. For both the following designs 'shells' were knitted.

For this design only remnants of yarn are used. Start each shell at the broad end. For this reason the jacket is knitted from the shoulder down. Prepare a paper pattern for the desired size. In this way you can lay the ever-increasing pieces onto it as you work so you can see what you have done and mark how the pieces are to be arranged.

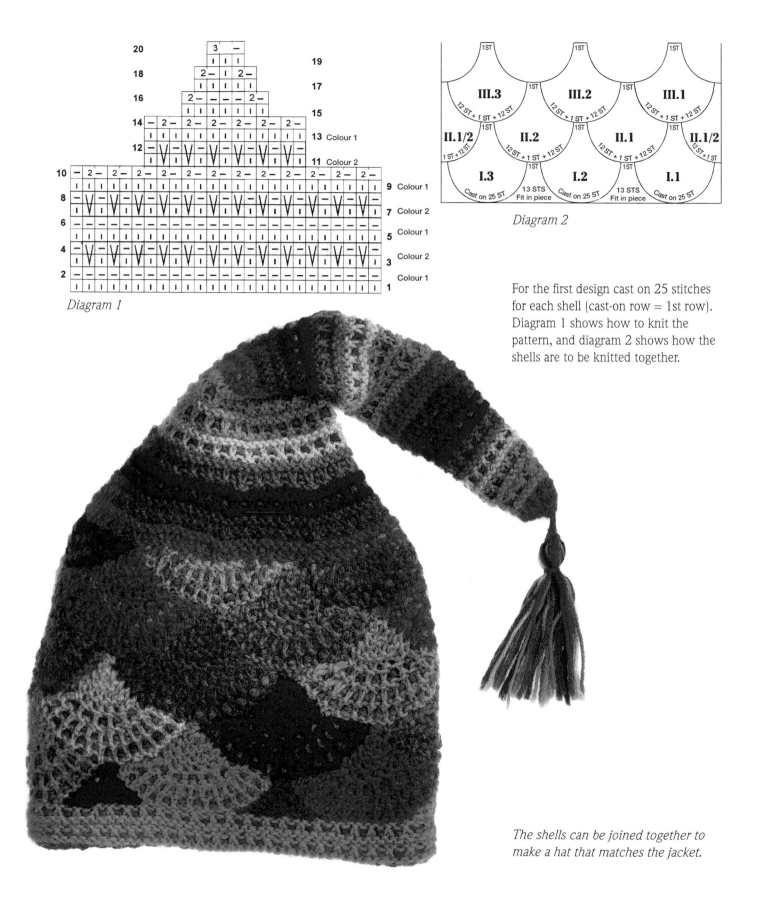

Diagram 1

Diagram 2

For the first design cast on 25 stitches for each shell (cast-on row = 1st row). Diagram 1 shows how to knit the pattern, and diagram 2 shows how the shells are to be knitted together.

The shells can be joined together to make a hat that matches the jacket.

For the second jacket an interesting colour effect is produced by the darker shade of colour 1, and the tapering-off of softer colours for colour 2. The diagram shows you how to knit a shell. The principle for knitting the pieces together (see diagram) is the same as for the first child's jacket. Except in this case only 31 stitches are cast on for the shells, and at the end 7 stitches are left. To join the shells, pick up 12 stitches from the round edges of each side of the existing shell, pick up 6 stitches from the space between the 7 cast-off stitches of the bottom of the shell which has already been knitted. Therefore, 3 shells are joined together, and half a pattern is worked for the side edges.

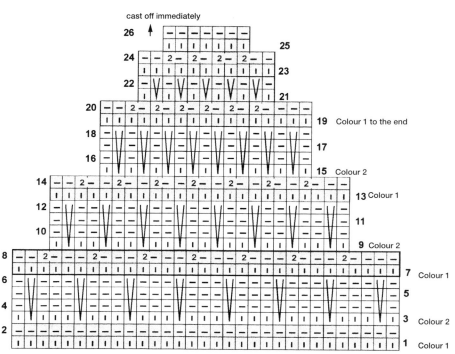

Explanation of the flowerpot

Begin the flower at the outer edge by casting on 64 stitches. The round shape is produced by decreasing stitches as the diagram shows. Note colour changes in rows 3 and 16. With the thread of the last stitch pick up 9 stitches on a needle on both sides, and cast off the stitches on a third needle on the front side. Finally, for the flowerpot, pick up 9 stitches from the outer edge of the flower. In this way the cast-off row forms the stem in the middle of the row. Knit 2 double rows purl in one colour, and 6 double rows moss stitch in another colour using these 9 stitches. Cast off in the last row.

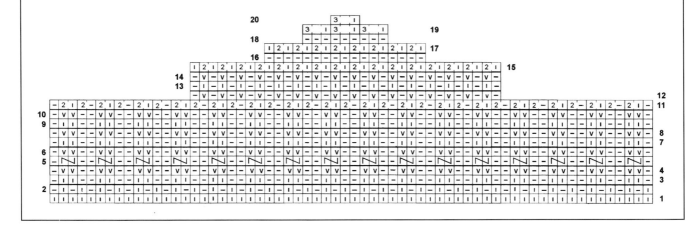

Acknowledgements

My grateful thanks go to the following people for their assistance with this book:

Henk and Henriette Beukers, who were the first people to recognise the novelty of my technique and who often published my patterns in the magazine "Ornamente", Franz Schlosser, who arranged invitations to fairs through the firm *Online* and so introduced me to the professional world.

My lady and gentlemen pupils who successfully used my idea of 'patchwork knitting' in their work.

All those knitters in distant countries who turned my ideas into beautiful garments by means of my explanations by letter.

To the knitters whose garments feature in this book: Elisabeth Beglinger and pupils, Barbara Borgmann, Vreni Fullemann, Karola Mahlkow, Wilhelma Naujok, Anette Raschke, Brigitte Schimkowiak, A. Schneiter (Anny Blatt), and Liane Schommertz.

All my former pupils who arranged workshops on their own to teach the techniques of 'patchwork knitting'.

The photo models Florian, Martin, Nina, Sarah, Rubin, Lion, Hanne and Niklas, as well as their parents.

My friend Norman Fisher who produced the manuscript with endless patience, often from illegible and incoherent text.

Manuela Juntke for the illustrations.

Gundula Steinart who worked on the copy.

Finally, to Saprotex International, who published this book.

I hope this book will help revive a beautiful, although rather neglected hobby, and also re-awaken the creativity in many people.

We all have talents – we only have to discover them.

Horst Schulz

List of suppliers

Normally any yarn is suitable to knit with Horst Schulz's technique. The garments shown in this book are mostly knitted with yarns from the firms

Online
Klaus Koch GmbH & Co. KG
Rheinstrasse, 35260 Stadtallendorf
Germany

Zürcher & Co
Lyssach, Postfach CH-3422 Kirchberg
Switzerland

Rowan
Representation for Germany:
Wool and Design

Rosmarie Kaufmann
Wolfshovener Strasse 76
52428 Jülich-Setternich
Germany

You can order complete kits of wool for Schulz models through:
Wolboutique Franz Schlosser
Albert-Schweitzer-Strasse 1
38226 Salzgitter
Germany

As a complement to this book you can order a video of the Horst Schulz knitting technique with his own models through
Häussner Wolle Handarbeiten
Am Lindenplatz 4
77652 Offenburg Germany

Also published by Saprotex International by Horst Schulz:
Patchwork Knitting for Adults

The author and publisher thank the firm Breitschwerdt Holzspielzeug for the kind support for the photographs.

Text-editing: Gundula Steinert, Leipzig
Correction of text: Margit Bogner
Photography: Annette Hempfling, Munich
Graphics/drawings: Manuela Junkte, Leipzig
Jacket design: Christa Manner, Munich
Layout: Walter Werbegrafik, Gundelfingen

Augusutus Verlag, Augsburg 1997
Copyright Weltbild Verlag GmbH, Augsburg
Published in English in 2000 by
Saprotex International (Pty) Ltd
PO Box 1293, East London, 5200, South Africa
Production & printing co-ordinator:
Unifoto International (Pty) Ltd
Printed in Singapore by Tien Wah Press Pte Ltd